Mormon and Moroni

written by Tiffany Thomas
illustrated by Nikki Casassa

CFI • An imprint of Cedar Fort, Inc. • Springville, Utah

HARD WORDS:
gold, Mormon, write

PARENT TIP: Explain that "some" does not use the silent e rule. Another exception is "come."

This is Mormon.
He is a man of God.

This is Moroni.
He is also a man
of God.

Mormon is Moroni's dad.
Moroni is Mormon's son.

Mormon writes the words
of God on the gold plates.

These are the Lamanites.

The Lamanites are very bad.
They slay all the good Nephites.

Mormon gives the plates to Moroni.

Mormon fights the
Lamanites and dies.

Moroni writes on the gold plates, too.

Moroni hides the gold plates
in a hill under a rock.

God keeps the gold plates safe.

The end.

ISBN 13: 978-1-4621-4337-5

Published by CFI, an imprint of Cedar Fort, Inc. • 2373 W. 700 S., Suite 100, Springville, UT 84663
Distributed by Cedar Fort, Inc., www.cedarfort.com

Cover design and interior layout design by Shawnda T. Craig
Cover design © 2022 Cedar Fort, Inc.
Printed in China • Printed on acid-free paper
10 9 8 7 6 5 4 3 2 1